# Sales Won't Save Your Small Business

---

## Focus on the TOP
## (Team, Offer, and Process)

**Joe Pardo**

www.SuperJoePardo.com

Joe Pardo
Joe@SuperJoePardo.com
(609) 868-9301
SuperJoePardo.com

ISBN: 9781791781255

Library of Congress: 2018900302

Editor: Tyler Tichelaar / Superior Book Productions
Cover Design & Interior Book Layout: Larry Alexander / Superior Book Productions
Author Photo: Joe Pardo

Every attempt has been made to source properly all quotes.

Printed in the United States of America

First Edition
1 2 3 4 5 6 7 8 9 10

**To Dominick and Joseph**

# Acknowledgments

N O BOOK IS written alone. I would like to thank my wife Melissa Pardo and daughter Ava Pardo for their love and support. Also, I would like to thank Lee Cockerell for his inspiration for this book, his foreword, his support, and his helping to make my childhood magical.

# Roadmap

**Foreword**
**by Lee Cockerell**

AM HAPPY TO recommend Joe Pardo's book, *Sales Won't Save Your Small Business.* That is the perfect title. Of course, we need sales to stay in business, but it's not the sales that matter so much as how you get those sales and how you keep them coming in and growing year afтer year that really matters. In my opinion, quality always wins out.

To be an excellent organization, you have to do every-thing right. In an excellent organization like Disney World, everything matters from the quality of the people we hire to intense training, testing, and enforcement, culminating in creating an environment and culture where everybody wakes up in the morning excited to come to work and a place where everybody matters and knows it. Do these things and you will trample the competition.

Joe has written the perfect recipe for creating the perfect product every time. Study this book, including answering the questions at the end of each chapter, and you will begin the journey to world class excellence.

Just remember to hire them right, train them right, and treat them right, and customers will flock to your doors. It's never too late to get better!

Lee Cockerell is the Retired Executive Vice President, Walt Disney World® Resort and Best-Selling Author of *Creating Magic: 10 Common Sense Leadership Strategies from a Life at Disney, The Customer Rules: The 39 Essential Rules for Delivering Sensational Customer Service, Time Management Magic: How to Get More Done Every Day*, and *Career Magic: How to Stay on Track to Achieve a Stellar Career*. Lee also produces a weekly fifteen-minute podcast on Leadership, Management, and Customer Service titled Creating Disney Magic. Before joining Disney in 1990 to open Disneyland Paris, Lee spent time in the US Army, eight years with Hilton Hotels, and seventeen years with Marriott International. Lee currently has a consulting, seminar, and public speaking company. For more

about Lee, go to his website, www.LeeCockerell.com.

# Introduction
## Can You Cut to the…

L ET'S CUT RIGHT to the chase. Sales are very important to every organization, but they will not save your business. Even at the most basic level, if you are losing money or breaking even on every sale, then you are building yourself a Titanic. Processes and relationships, however, will not only save your business, but put it on the path to accelerated growth!

Sales are the lifeblood of business, but having more sales will not solve the issues that come along with growth. Plenty of excuses can be made for why a business is not reaching its full potential or even failing. If you are stuck in a sales cycle of selling unprofitable goods or services, you may have difficulty digging yourself out of that hole. However, refining your processes to reduce your costs can help you continue selling those low-profit goods and services while making a profit. That said, changing your sales cycle will become more complex when you start looking at low-profit offerings as loss leaders for the business.

But don't worry. You're looking for answers to these problems, which is why you've picked up this book. *Sales Won't Save Your Small Business* is written for every business owner, man-ager, supervisor, and team leader who has ever felt stressed out and frustrated because of his or her business. Sales are not everything when it comes to business growth and success. As with people, businesses need to grow in more ways than one.

In these pages we're going to focus on the TOP: Team, Offer, and Process. Each of those three items will be the focus of one part of this book. Overall, by focusing your attention on these three areas, you will learn to:

1. Identify what is truly important to you.

2. Understand and use your numbers for accelerated growth.

3. Plus-up your current offering.

4. Improve your inventory management.

5. Better handle perception management.

6. Create a consistent experience.

7. Integrate technology.

8. Create predictable processes.

9. Balance sales.

10. Implement scheduling.

11. Define your vision for success.

Before you read further, I want you to think about the following questions. Take a few minutes and write down your answers to them.

Why did you start your business?

_____

_____

_____

_____

_____

What do you love about your business?

_____

_____

_____

_____

_____

What is the biggest stress generator in your business?

_____

_____

_____

_____

_____

Finally, I want you to understand that this book is designed to be as concise as possible. I write books for people like me who do not like to read books. That is why this book is straight, to the point, with large font, short specific chapters, and no filler text. I wipe away the limitations that hold people like me back from reading books in the first place.

Speaking of chapters, you may have noticed the Contents page is titled "Roadmap" and each chapter is titled "pin." I want you to think of this book as your roadmap to success. Each pin represents a destination on that roadmap where you can fuel up on wisdom you need to reach success. At the conclusion of each pin, you will find a few questions. The questions are designed to give you time to reflect on what you have learned. The first question allows you to give yourself a 1-10 rating on how well you feel you are doing in a particular area. The second and sometimes third question enables you to think about what an ideal situation looks like to you. The final question is meant for you to take action and report back on your findings. This means you will need to check your ego at the door in order to get the most helpful answers from yourself and your team. The goal is for you to discover things you did not realize about others, a particular situation, and yourself. Afterwards, I invite you to post the pin numbers, questions, and your answers to social media with #saleswontsave so everyone can learn from one another.

I want you to be able to read and learn, and then get out there and start implementing the lessons into your business!

Are you ready to take your business to the next level? Then let's begin!

# Part 1
# Focus on the Team

# Pin 1
## How Do I Empower Myself?

YOU CANNOT TAKE care of others around you effectively if you do not lead by example and take care of yourself first. Similar to the emergency oxygen masks on airplanes, you need to put your mask on first before helping others. Having better self-care will lead to a happier and more productive you. Obtaining a clearer mind will lead to a better vision for your business. Some of the biggest aspects of self-care that people neglect are sleep, maintaining relationships, and making time.

When it comes to sleep, are you getting enough? Being trapped in an endless cycle of not getting enough sleep has plenty of side effects. Reduced concentration and a reduced immune system are two big results from sleep loss that I've seen business owners fall victim to all too often. You must be awake, alert, and present to be able to make the best decisions for you and your business. Getting sick because of a weak-ened immune system is only going to reduce your time and effectiveness when working on and in your business.

I use a sleep calculator and alarm to make sure I am getting optimal amounts of sleep. Your body goes through sleep cycles that take ninety minutes to complete. When you wake up in the middle of a sleep cycle, then you will wake up more tired than when you went to sleep. Obviously, many factors decide whether we can sleep right up to the end of a sleep cycle. You can get an app on your smartphone that will help you calculate the proper time to go to bed and wake up.

Make the extra effort to ensure you are going to sleep as early as possible so you can wake up earlier. You will be amazed by how much you can accomplish when you wake up at the end of a sleep cycle and jump right into work. If I go to bed about 9:30 p.m., and take about fourteen minutes to fall asleep, I am able to wake up at 3:44 a.m. after six hours of sleep (four complete cycles), 5:14 a.m. after seven-and-a-half hours of sleep (five complete cycles), or 6:44 a.m. after nine hours of sleep (six complete cycles). I understand that going to bed earlier can be tough to do at first, but just like with anything, practice makes perfect. You need to be intentional with your time to get the most out of every minute.

Maintaining personal relationships is key in making sure you have a balanced life. The range goes from spending time with family and friends to evaluating current relationships. To have a healthy balance of work and social interaction, you need to cut out the toxic relationships. Relationships that result in a constant drain on your time or resources need to be discontinued. Finding the give and take within a relationship is the key to helping you achieve balance in your social life and, more importantly, your time.

Twenty-four hours is the gift we receive every single morning. Every person on this planet receives the same number of hours. You need to make sure you are using every minute to its fullest potential. We all have a limited amount of time, so if we squander too many seconds, minutes, hours, days, weeks, months, years, or decades, we will not achieve what we are in this life to do. This is not about hustling all of the time but, more importantly, constantly evaluating how you are spending your time because it is the most valuable and most limited resource you have.

Making time for self-care is often incredibly neglected by business owners and managers. This neglect can happen especially when you get the feeling that if you are not working, you are not making money or being productive. In the business' beginning stages, that will almost always be true, but as your business grows, you need to remember that you need to grow too! Become intentional about setting aside time for family, friends, self-reflection, hobbies, recovering, relaxing, daydreaming, doctor visits, and more.

*Super Joe Says:*
*Build your business for your lifestyle,*
*not your lifestyle for your business.*

Giving yourself the time, space, and permission to be self-aware and self-evaluate is one of the most important aspects of empowering yourself. You will enable yourself to find what reset switches you have. Reset switches enable you to go from stressed out to relaxed in a short amount of time. My reset switches include taking a nap, watching some funny videos, and taking deep breaths. Remembering to breathe will help you have a clear vision of the tasks at hand.

Many will tell you that you constantly need to hustle your face off. That approach will ultimately lead to grinding away at your business and your life. I constantly have to remind myself that Rome was not built in a day, and I cannot accomplish everything all at once. The greatest of goals almost always need to be achieved at different milestones in your progress. It is important to know when getting less sleep and working twenty hours or more in a row is appropriate. Do not let yourself get sucked into working endless work days all of the time. Use your ability to hustle endlessly as a tool, rather than a strategy.

*Super Joe Says:*

*When the chips are down, you need to swing the bat.*

Becoming self-aware allows you to ask questions about yourself. Give yourself permission to look at how others interact with you. Then you can begin to make adjustments to how your interact with others. Do not be afraid to ask trusted friends and family members for input on how your actions, words, and mannerisms play a part in how they interact with you. Be honest with yourself when trying to find solutions to the small things that may be holding you back in life and in business. Keep in mind that the small things add up to the big picture and make the biggest impact. At the same time, when you ask for input from others, it is the perfect time to work on your listening skills.

Listening skills are some of the best skills you can exhibit to others. In life and in business, your listening skills are more important than your ability to talk and sell. The ability to listen and reflect back what others are communicating to you will take your relationships, life, and business to new heights. When reflecting back to others, work on being really precise in the questions you ask—questions that will cause the other person to pause and give a deeper answer. The deeper the answer you receive, the deeper the connection you will have, and the better you will be able to grow the relationship.

*Super Joe Says:*
*You must take care of yourself first*
*before you can take care of others.*

Finally, I want you to be intentional with your time in a way that displays to others that you are present in the moment. We all get sucked into our smartphones from time to time. When someone is asking for your attention, make sure you are giving it. Looking down at your phone communicates that you are too busy to listen to what the other person is offering. If you need to ask for a moment to finish what you are doing, then ask for it. Being direct with your intentions and time displays your respect for other people and their time.

You may be wondering what all this has to do with business? Well, your relationships and how you communicate with people have everything to do with business. We will look at that in more detail in the next pin, but first, take a moment to reflect upon what you've learned in this pin and how it can move you forward in your goals.

**Exercise**

On a scale of 1 to 10 (10 being the best): Are you getting enough sleep at night? If your answer is lower than a 6, how can you improve this situation?

_____

_____

_____

_____

_____

_____

Where can you find more time in your day to accomplish more or to relax more? What is an ineffective use of your time that you can eliminate?

_____

_____

_____

_____

_____

_____

_____

Make a concerted effort to listen to someone today and ask specific questions when you reflect back to him or her. What did you learn from this experience? Did it make your relationship better?

_____

_____

_____

_____

_____

_____

*Don't forget to post the pin numbers, questions, and your answers to social media with #saleswontsave so everyone can learn from one another.*

## Pin 2
## How Is Every Business a Relationship Business?

RELATIONSHIPS ARE THE foundation of every single business, no matter whether it is a service- or product-based business. Your business is a tree, and the roots of that tree are made of strong relationships. It doesn't matter whether we are talking about relationships with your customers, your team, your industry, or your community. There is no getting around the fact that the relationships you, your team, and your business forge will lay the groundwork for growth and success.

Even completely online businesses have other tools at their disposal to build relationships; those tools are just built on a different foundation than face to face. No matter what kind of business you have, you must stay competitive with excellent customer service, shipping, packaging, website design, marketing, product offerings, and pricing to build brand loyalty. Customer service is essential for any business, and maintaining a consistent feel through all of the touchpoints with your customers can be a challenge. Having the correct processes in place for training your team is crucial to delivering consistency. Also, be mindful to allow enough flexibility to prevent policy from getting in the way of making customers happy. In most cases, your touchpoints with your customers are not nearly as personable as having a one-on-one relationship with each customer. The goal is to build out each touchpoint to give customers the illusion of dealing with a person.

Many paths will build relationships with your customers—even if they are just clicking some buttons on a web browser to purchase from you. Start with marketing your brand in a way that will build a relationship with your target audience. Your branding can include a social mission that does good in the world while making customers feel good about working with you.

*Super Joe Says:*

*Society starts with you.*

My consulting company, 234 Solutions, has a social mission of not only creating but also saving jobs. We back that up by donating a percentage of our profits to Hopeworks 'N Camden (www.Hopeworks.org) to help empower and train the youth of Camden, New Jersey, to be able to enter the workforce or start their own businesses.

Hosting events for your customers can help them increase their knowledge and grow their networks in unpredictable ways. They'll remember how you benefited them, which will strengthen your bond with them, and that will, in turn, increase your market reach. Hosted events can include training sessions, networking meetups for your industry, conventions, conferences, or vendor showrooms with time to meet with industry representatives and experts.

A strong relationship builder in my family's business, Pardo's Truck Service Parts Warehouse, Inc., was our annual Fleet Parts Show hosted every February on the Wednesday right after Valentine's Day. This one-night event would start around 3 p.m. and run until 10 p.m. During that time, close to

1,000 attendees would make their way through a large show-room of parts manufacturers' displays. Once through the showroom full of manufacturer representatives, their products, endless catalogs, freebies, giveaways, and showroom displays, the attendees would be greeted with a large buffet with premium food choices and a free open bar. The event was our way of saying thank you to our customers and their families, while fishing for more business. We also had classes put on by the manufacturer representatives and nearly endless door prizes that we gave away. If you set up your events correctly, you should be able to capitalize on them in multiple ways, and not just from getting more business out of the customers who come to the event. By bringing so many businesses together, you will be putting yourself in the driver's seat for negotiating bigger and better deals. These events will help give you leverage and display your dominance in your industry and market area.

Networking with potential customers is a great way to start building relationships. Finding or creating events so you can meet others is great, but also consider sponsoring outside events. Having a captive audience helps people become familiar with your business and recognize your brand. Then you can move from building awareness to building relationships with potential customers. To build a winning networking and relationship-building formula, always be in a position to give more than you expect or even receive. You would be surprised by how far simple gestures of picking up a breakfast sandwich, donuts, holding doors, being courteous, making a connection for someone to another person, or just understanding how to have a conversation can positively impact your bottom line.

When it comes to competition, keep in mind that your competition may actually be your ally in a different sector of business. While Apple and Samsung compete for consumers to buy their phones, Samsung is also a partner of Apple's and makes LCD screens for the iPhone. Don't worry too much about your competition. Instead, focus on improving you, your team, your customer's experience, and your business. Copying your competition will likely not lead you to your destination.

The dirty "C" word, Communication, while difficult, is the backbone for any relationship to work, and in business, that is no exception. Regularly engaging with others with open lines of communication is a winning strategy every time. No matter whether it is with other team members or customers, if you are not communicating, you are not doing your job. Identifying breakdowns in communication is the quickest way to gain trust, customers, revenue, profit, more time, a better reputation, and better team members.

Now that you know why building relationships is so important, you need to get your team onboard to help you, but first, let's reflect and apply what we learned.

**Exercise**

On a scale of 1 to 10 (10 being the best): Do you feel you have strong business relationships? Can you name three of your strong business relationships? What makes them stronger than others?

_____

_____

_____

_____

_____

_____

_____

_____

_____

_____

_____

Can you describe what a good business relationship looks like to you?

_____

_____

_____

_____

_____

_____

_____

_____

_____

_____

_____

_____

_____

_____

_____

_____

_____

Reach out to someone you have a weak business relationship with. Find out what you can do to strengthen the bond. After you have reached out, what is one thing you now see you can improve upon to strengthen this and other business relationships?

_____

_____

_____

_____

_____

_____

_____

_____

_____

_____

_____

_____

_____

_____

_____

_____

*Don't forget to post the pin numbers, questions, and your answers to social media with #saleswontsave so everyone can learn from one another.*

# Pin 3
# How Do I Empower My Team?

I REFER TO EMPLOYEES as team members. It may sound cheesy, but I believe in empowering others to be the best versions of themselves. People feel more connected to a cause when they feel they add value to a system. Equally, they need to feel valued as part of the team. As with any team, there is a place for leaders and captains (managers, project leaders, etc.). Giving your team members the opportunity to move up and have more responsibilities is important because it makes them want to give more to the cause and be vested in it. Plenty of times, I have been shocked by how team members have devoted their time and energy to projects they believed in.

First, as the leader, you need to lead by example. This goes without saying, but just like with setting the expectations for the team, it is nice to get a refresher. Never expect anyone on your team to do something you wouldn't be willing to do yourself. What comes with that territory is knowing how long each and every person on your team takes to complete the tasks assigned to his or her position. As a leader, you should know from the start whether someone is milking the task he or she is given. If you have not done the work yourself, you have no baseline to know how long it should take someone who is new or old on the team to complete assigned tasks.

A great way to have a better understanding of what your team does is to send out a survey every year. This way you will be able to track the development of each position in the organization. It will give you better insight into what needs to be covered when a team member is absent or departs the team.

Second, as the leader, it is up to you to set expectations for the relationship. Unmet expectations are the quickest way for things to turn sour in your team. It is imperative, therefore, that right out of the gate, you let your team members know exactly what you expect from them in terms of work and conduct. Then no discussion is needed later about miscommunications or misunderstandings. If you don't know what you expect out of your team, then take some time to sit back and figure out what those expectations are.

Expectations need to be laid out over a set period of time. To expect everyone to receive your message after the first sit down is short-sighted. Be prepared to raise the bar of expectations over the course of a few weeks. Doing so will net the best results and weed out any team members who just refuse to conform to what is expected of the team.

Third, you need to build your team's structure. If you want your team members to feel like they have something to work for and earn, then there has to be a structure (ladder) for them to move up to. Just like with sports teams, different positions are needed to accomplish the business' goals. It is up to you to define those positions. Besides determining salaries for each position, figure out how much salary will make up your overall company budget. How can that budget be maintained while allowing you to remain competitive in the job market? Structure is also important when accounting for people not coming to work. If someone takes a vacation, gets sick, or quits, a chain of command is needed so everyone knows how, where, and when to step in. I'll delve more into how to create this structure when I discuss processes in Pin 16: How Do I Create Profitable and Predictable Processes?

Finally, and most importantly, you need to show appreciation for the work your team does. Sometimes, verbalizing appreciation is enough, but you should look for other ways to show your appreciation. Offering paid benefits that go above and beyond what your competition is offering for the position can be crucial in acquiring the best talent, and in retaining that talent because your team members feel appreciated. Tickets to events with no strings attached, occasionally purchasing lunch for your team, or even cash bonuses based on set goals are great ways to show appreciation. The possibilities for showing appreciation are endless; just make sure you are doing it if you want to grow and develop your team. Otherwise, you will constantly be turning over your team and wondering why you don't have a dedicated, steady staff.

*Super Joe Says:*

*Treat others how you want to be treated,*

*until you know how they want to be treated.*

Treat your team like a team! You need to encourage your team members along the way to ensure their growth both personally and professionally. As a community member, it is part of your duty to leave your fellow community members in better shape than when they became part of your team.

Empower your team to make decisions. Not every decision can, will, and should be made by team members, but set your team members up to make decisions for themselves. Part of growth is gaining experience, and the only way to gain experience is to make decisions. Both good and bad decisions will enable your team members to grow beyond the skill sets and knowledge they brought to the team.

Look into hosting team-building exercises, or even hosting events where your team can bond and grow together. Generally, you will have more success if you close your business early for these events. Be aware that if you plan to have events after work hours, some team members may not be able to attend. You need to understand and respect that others might not have the lifestyle you live. To expect them to do after-hours activities can add stress to your team members' lives, especially if it is impossible for them to make the events. You could be pushing a great teammate right out the door without even realizing it by alienating him or her.

Consider incentivizing team growth with gift cards, tickets to events, or other prizes. Try to make it feasible for the rewards to be given to the whole team. The goal is not to create divisiveness among team members. I have lived through such divisive situations and can tell you that, ultimately, they are detrimental for retaining team members. Instead, use your resources to bring rewards to the table that cost you nothing. Try to reach out to sales reps and ask them for kickbacks to reward your team members for accomplishing goals using Next Gen Numbers. I will explain more about Next Gen Numbers and how to utilize them in Pin 22.

While your customers are not employed by you, it is important to remind them that they employ you and your team. Find ways to empower them so they will choose to continue as your customers. One way to do that is through training classes. Having an educated customer base will not only empower them to make good decisions for their own businesses, but position you and your team as leaders in the area and industry.

Now you know how to empower your team, but that's only part of being an effective leader. Let's review what we learned in this pin, and then we'll look at effective leadership in more detail.

**Exercise**

On a scale of 0-10 (10 being the best): How well do you feel you empower your team members? Explain why you gave yourself that score.

_____

_____

_____

_____

_____

_____

_____

_____

_____

Describe the ways you are currently empowering your team members. In what ways would you ideally like to empower them?

_____

_____

_____

_____

_____

_____

_____

_____

Encourage discussion with your team members about empowerment and the ways they feel they would be best-empowered. Afterwards, write down at least one thing you can improve upon to empower your team members and your relationships with them.

_____

_____

_____

_____

_____

_____

_____

_____

_____

_____

*Don't forget to post the pin numbers, questions, and your answers to social media with #saleswontsave so everyone can learn from one another.*

# Pin 4
# How Can I Become a More Effective Leader?

I BELIEVE THE BEST way to become a more effective leader is to start with becoming self-aware. Self-evaluating how you treat yourself and the world around you can be a very eye-opening experience; in fact, you may not like what you discover. Regardless, you'll be able to start identifying your strengths and weaknesses. Understanding your strengths and weaknesses will help you better understand how you can help lead others.

*Super Joe Says:*

*Always lead by example.*

Respect is earned and not given. As a leader, you must constantly be willing to dig in and do the work yourself. At times, you will need to fill in because of a worker shortage or an emergency. In such situations, it is important for your team members to understand you are not just going to sit back and make them do all the work. This does not mean, however, that you should be working *in* your business all of the time versus *on* your business. A great leader knows how to find the balance that will earn respect. You also should be aware that not every team member will understand the supervisor's role on the team. Many times, it is behind-the-scenes work that enables supervisors to keep their positions.

Still, never be afraid to roll up your sleeves and dig in. Do not expect the team you lead to do jobs you would not want to do yourself. If you find yourself in that position, maybe you should be looking for a new position or business altogether. Rolling up your sleeves is vital because, as a leader, you should know the tasks of each and every team member who operates under you—the key reason being that when you know how long every task for every position takes and what it encompasses, you will understand the pitfalls that happen and be better able to help resolve them. Furthermore, understanding every task enables you to have a better grip on how to optimize efficiently for your team going forward. Your team members may not understand how each position interacts with the others throughout a day, week, month, or year, but as the leader who has experienced it all, you will.

When seeking to become a better leader, understand that trying to be a "nice boss" is not the answer; instead, look for ways to become more empathetic. Placing yourself in others' shoes and seeing things from their perspectives will enable you to customize how you interact with each team member. Being empathetic will give the appearance of being that "nice boss" without becoming a doormat in the process. Keep in mind that multiple perspectives exist for every story; you need to be able to analyze them to pick the best solution to every problem. There is always a way; you just need to be willing to look hard enough to find the solution.

As a leader, you need to check your ego at the door and find ways to be as selfless as possible. Becoming as relatable as possible will allow your team to look at you as a leader and not someone who is just privileged. No matter what your situation, being able to find ways to remain relatable through your actions and words will give others confidence in your ability. Actions always speak louder than words, so being able to treat others the way they would like to be treated will take you a lot further in reaching your team and company goals. Remember, you always catch more flies with honey than vinegar.

Earlier, I stated that a business is a tree and the relationships are the roots. If you're a good leader, you'll have strong, healthy roots, branches, leaves, and a trunk. After we reflect on what we learned in this pin, in the next pin we'll look at the structure of the tree itself.

## Exercise

On a scale of 0-10 (10 being the best): How well do you feel you are able to self-evaluate and be self-aware? If you do not self-evaluate, why not?

_____

_____

_____

_____

_____

_____

Describe a situation where you were able to grow afterwards

thanks to self-evaluating yourself and your choices. How do

you feel self-evaluation will be helpful to you going forward?

_____

_____

_____

_____

_____

_____

_____

_____

_____

_____

_____

Describe a situation and the choices you made in the situation. How do you feel your choices affected others? Ask someone you trust who knows the situation for honest feedback on how you handle specific situations. How does this person's feedback line up with what you wrote down?

_____

_____

_____

_____

_____

_____

_____

_____

_____

_____

_____

_____

*Don't forget to post the pin numbers, questions, and your answers to social media with #saleswontsave so everyone can learn from one another.*

# Pin 5
# How Is a Business a Tree?

ONE COMMENT I have always disliked hearing is, "Must be nice." When I was growing up, I often heard this response whenever my family business came up in conversation. The idea that as an owner or boss, it must be nice not to have anyone above you keeping tabs on your actions is absurd, misguided, and dangerous. To understand why, let's look at how a business is like a tree.

An organizational chart, with all of the positions laid out top to bottom, should be looked at as a tree. Customers are the sunlight and the water needed for the tree to thrive. The marketplace is the soil in which the tree operates to gather water and sunlight. The roots are the company's team members who are bringing in sales to maintain the tree's foundation in the soil. The trunk is the administration, which does not bring in customers, but protects the tree's structure, allowing it to grow. The leaves are the high-end customers who allow the organization to soak up the sun's rays. These customers are captured through networking with other organizations' top team members, such as CEOs.

*Super Joe Says:*
*Take care of your tree,*
*and it will take care of you.*

If the water and sunlight are taken away from the tree, it will start to wither and die. Just because you operate your own business does not mean you do not have a boss. The bosses are the customers because if they stop coming to you, your business will die just like a tree without water or sunlight.

I want you to give consideration to your company's organization: whom you have assigned to the positions, and how you can best support them to grow your tree as strong, high, and wide as possible. After the following exercise, we will discuss how training for your team can help increase your profit.

## Exercise

On a scale of 0-10 (10 being the best): How well do you feel your business' team is organized? Explain why you gave this score.

_____

_____

_____

_____

_____

_____

_____

_____

Ideally, how do you feel your business could be better organized for maximum growth and efficiency?

_____

_____

_____

---

---

---

---

---

---

Discuss with your team how your business tree is laid out. Did you find anything missing from the tree that would be beneficial? Describe some possible solutions for fixing the missing pieces.

---

---

---

---

---

---

_____

_____

_____

_____

_____

*Don't forget to post the pin numbers, questions, and your answers to social media with #saleswontsave so everyone can learn from one another.*

**Pin 6**
**How Can I Grow My Profit Through Training?**

TRAINING IS ALSO crucial to growing, retaining, and developing your team. How can you expect your team members to succeed if they have not had proper training on how you expect work to be completed? Remember, you have to set expectations right out of the gate. Giving the proper training from the start means that you have a process in place to set your team members up to win.

*Super Joe Says:*

*Teach them to win.*

Of course, it doesn't end there; you need to continue training throughout their time with your business. Having routine training is important because it gives your team the opportunity to adjust to the tweaks you make to your processes and to refresh old skills. It can also go a long way toward helping with cross-training so that when people aren't able to make it into work, you don't miss a beat and your team members feel like they can stay on top of the tasks needed to get by during the worker shortage.

The importance of training can be very easy to overlook, and forgetting to perform it often enough will prevent your team from remaining sharp. For that reason, it's important to set time aside in your schedule to plan for upcoming training for your team. Your ability to train new and old team members will be crucial in creating a consistent experience for your team and for your customers.

With all of the training comes increased responsibility for your team members. After you reflect on how you are making sure your team is getting ample training, we will dive into how to let power go to your well-trained team to expedite growth.

**Exercise**

On a scale of 0-10 (10 being the best): How well do you feel your business is training its team? Why did you give that score?

_____

_____

_____

_____

_____

_____

_____

_____

_____

_____

What are some areas in which you feel your business does well in training? Conversely, what areas do you feel your team needs to improve upon in its training?

_____

_____

_____

_____

_____

_____

_____

_____

_____

Discuss your current training situation with your team members to gather feedback on what they would like training to cover. Write and compare their thoughts on training with what you would ideally like to see done for training.

_____

_____

_____

_____

_____

_____

_____

_____

_____

_____

_____

*Don't forget to post the pin numbers, questions, and your answers to social media with #saleswontsave so everyone can learn from one another.*

# Pin 7
## Do I Have the Power to Let Power Go?

MAKING A DECISION and allowing that decision to grow or to die is important for your growth as a leader and for the growth of your business. Becoming a larger business requires you to relinquish power through proper training, refining your process, and empowering your team.

*Super Joe Says:*
*The only thing in this world that is truly yours*
*is your word.*

When you make the decision to micromanage your team, you are taking power away from your managers. This diminishes the role of your managers and makes team members second-guess their managers' judgment and decisions. Your team members will start to do things in accordance with what they believe you, the owner, will want instead of allowing management to do its job.

If your team members get the sense that you do not have faith in your managers' decisions, they will lose both trust and respect for their managers. This situation creates the risk that your decisions will not be followed through on because your managers are an extension of your decisions, plans, and processes, but your team members may not believe their managers' directives have come down from you. You still need to hold your managers accountable, but do not let yourself discipline or show frustration with your managers in front of your team members. If a manager is going to do something to lose the team's trust and respect, let it come from the manager and not from you showing a lack of trust and respect for the manager in front of the team. Open communication should always be strived for with all of your team, but especially with managers.

To ensure you regularly have open lines of communication, schedule team members to meet weekly and one-on-

one with their supervisors. Regular meetings are a great way to take the edge off and remove the guesswork when it comes to understanding how your team members are feeling. It also gives everyone an opportunity to address known issues and come up with solutions for them. Such meetings will also allow team members to address any issues they are having one-on-one so they feel heard.

One pitfall of running a multi-location business is that, as the owner, you may be tempted to start micromanaging at the location closest to where you reside or where you have your main office. You have to stay on top of yourself to make sure you are creating blanketing processes that fit the entire business' needs rather than just hounding the team you see and work with every day. Remember, you need to be willing to let power go if you are ever going to grow your business to the level of your pre-set growth goals and beyond. Don't waste your energy and, more importantly, your time sweating the small stuff. Work with your management team to create processes for handling the little things so they do not become big problems down the road. You need all of the time, energy, and space you can find to create your business' future.

Having your team, management team, and processes implemented effectively is what will allow you to work on your business, rather than in your business.

*Super Joe Says:*
*Be prepared to take steps backward*
*in order to make giant leaps forward.*

You can make a change in leadership without taking a step backward in the business. That is why it's so important (I cannot emphasize this enough) to empower all of your team every step of the way. Two ways to ensure you are properly empowering your team is through communication and choosing the right teammates in the first place. We'll look at how to choose those teammates in the next three pins.

**Exercise**

On a scale of 0-10 (10 being the best): How well do you feel
you are able to distribute power to others? Why did you give
yourself that score?

_____

_____

_____

_____

_____

_____

_____

_____

In which areas do you feel you could distribute power away
from yourself? Which areas do you feel would be tough to
distribute to others?

_____

_____

_____

_____

_____

_____

_____

_____

_____

_____

Discuss the current distribution of power with your team members. Ask them how they could help in taking on more power. What are the reasons for and against each of the proposed power shifts?

_____

_____

_____

_____

_____

_____

_____

*Don't forget to post the pin numbers, questions, and your answers to social media with #saleswontsave so everyone can learn from one another.*

# Pin 8
## How Do I Build My Team?

BEFORE YOU CAN start effectively hiring team members, you have to decide which positions are needed, wanted, and required to complete goals. Spending time in the processes of your business is critical to knowing whether a position is required for the business to function. It will also reveal whether the position is needed at all or whether it is convenient for you and your team to rely on the position.

Determining what positions are needed can be accomplished by going through each and every role in your organization and asking, "What tasks do you take care of in a normal week?" Don't be surprised if some team members become defensive when posed with this question. To ward off such a reaction, make sure you are clear with them about your intentions. In order to strengthen your business and provide more jobs in the world, you have to know exactly what each role in your business holds. You may find out that the roles you set up for people to play are less than half of what they actually wind up doing in the business.

Knowing what is actually going on in the business on a team member level is eye-opening. "Knowing is half the battle!" Knowledge will allow you to make informed decisions that can alter your company's course. In the next part, we will get into process building so you can create more focus for your team members' various positions and roles.

## How Do I Choose My Team?

As in any good heist movie, it is crucial to be picky in your team member selection process. The selection starts, of course, by actually having a process for selection in place. The process you create is critical for making sure you are not wasting time, energy, and resources on people who do not fit into the model you are building.

As the owner, it is part of your job to make sure you are designing your team-building process for success. Incorporate something that sets you apart from other businesses in your industry. An example could be that in your job listing, you ask applicants to answer a simple question that fits into your culture. For example, "When was the last time you made someone smile, and what did you do to make that happen?" You will be surprised by how many applicants will ignore a simple instruction and just send in their resumes. Those people have already disqualified themselves. As for those who answer the question, if the question is important enough to the culture you are trying to create, then the responses will help you easily avoid hiring the wrong people.

Also keep in mind that when you hire someone, that person may stay with you for a long time. Therefore, it's important to ask questions in the interview that pertain to past shifts in your business or industry. Hiring coachable and flexible talent is a must to ensure that when things change in your company or industry, including with technology, your team can productively and proactively handle the changes.

*Super Joe Says:*

*Loyalty and understanding go a long way*

*toward completing goals.*

## What Do I Do When It Doesn't Work Out?

Your decisions on positions and team members will not always work out in the business' favor. From the start, you need to make sure you are giving the support and tools required for your team to succeed. What kind of support and tools will be revealed when you start talking with your team members about what they do within the company? Once you have that knowledge, you need to be willing to ask more questions and eventually act on what makes sense and cents.

When the time comes to make a decision about letting someone go from a position, you need to consider all perspectives. You may find that someone who has been loyal to your organization may just need a new role. People change over time, and what is going on in their personal lives might be taking a toll on their happiness and productivity. Try to see whether a better fit exists for the person elsewhere in your business. That way you do not have to let someone go, and you may be able to fill a need in your business that requires knowledge of the industry and would be hard to fill from the outside.

How you go about structuring pay, benefits, and hours will also play a huge role when someone decides to stay or depart. Never forget that loyal people are hard to come by.

*Super Joe Says:*

*Don't panic.*

When faced with a crisis, such as having a key team member leave the company, it is easy to lose sight of the business you have built and the service you provide to your customers. The systems and processes you have built are vital for keeping your customers satisfied, regardless of whether a team member is ready to leave your team.

Your service offering should be set at a high level and set up in a predictable manner. The loss of one team member should not disrupt your business. Your customers should not miss a beat because you have a position that needs to be filled. Sometimes that means you need to roll up your sleeves and fill in, but the processes you have created should make it easy to plug someone into the position quickly and seamlessly.

Cause for concern can come into play if one of your team members leaves your company to go work for a competitor. While it is possible this person could take some business away from your organization, you need to stay focused that you have built a model that takes care of the customer. Ultimately, that is what people buy into when they are making purchases from your business. Consider that a customer may only want to deal with a specific team member. When that team member changes her place of employment, the customer follows her, thus changing where he does business. However, if the customer perceives the purchasing system where the team member has gone as being radically different, cumbersome, or a headache, that customer will not stick around for long. Again, stay focused on what you have built and what you are currently building for both your team and customers.

The number one way to make customers happy so they will stick around is through consistency. When you bring consistency to the table, customers are able to get comfortable. Over time, being comfortable will turn into confidence, and that confidence will stick around a lot longer than any single team member likely will. When building out the processes for your team to go through, it's important to make sure they stick to them. Allowing certain employees to buck the system and get their way is a short-term win for the customer and the team member, but a long-term loss for the system, team, and overall business.

Building the necessary systems and processes as you grow ensures that you don't wind up with lots of long-term employees who are stuck in the "old way" of getting things done. Many times, the "old way" is not even a process anyone else uses. When a specific process works for a team member, regardless of whether it is an approved process, he or she will keep doing it.

The path of least resistance winds up being the best way to get things done. When left unchecked or unquestioned, these solo processes can wind up costing the business lots of money, time, and headache on behalf of other team members who are following the rules.

So how do you resolve this "old process" situation if it already exists? That's the subject of our next pin.

**Exercise**

On a scale of 0-10 (10 being the best): Overall, how do you feel your team does with putting the right people in the right positions? Why did you choose that score?

_____

_____

_____

_____

_____

_____

_____

_____

_____

_____

Which positions would you like to create if there were no limiting factors? Do you feel you have a good process in place to find the right talent for each position?

_____

_____

_____

_____

_____

_____

_____

_____

Discuss with your team members how they feel about the positions they fill on the team. What reasons did you come up with for and against adding more positions to your team?

_____

_____

_____

_____

_____

_____

_____

_____

_____

_____

_____

_____

_____

_____

*Don't forget to post the pin numbers, questions, and your answers to social media with #saleswontsave so everyone can learn from one another.*

# Pin 9
# What Makes Perception, Reality?

MANY OF YOU reading this book probably have long-term team members. Teaching new systems and processes to long-term team members can be a daunting task. Some will get on board with making changes for the better, but many may not want to make the necessary changes, especially if their perception of the new process is that it will make their jobs more difficult, regardless of whether that is true.

*Super Joe Says:*

*See the perception of your business through the lens of others first; then you can start to raise the perception.*

Those unwilling to adapt and change will likely become a cancer in your organization. Over time, this cancer can pull apart your business' culture, mentality, and team.

Even worse, the perception your team has can seep into your customer base. The way your team communicates with customers is key to ensuring a consistent experience. If your team starts changing the language it uses to or around customers, that poor perception will start to become the customer's perception. An example of this could be one of your team members saying to himself or another team member while in front of a customer, "We never have anything in stock anymore." Customers should never be subjected to negative talk about the company they are relying on to deliver service. The customer may start to believe what he is hearing regardless of how opinionated a statement may be or who it comes from.

Perception management is crucial for success, especially when it comes to changes in a business. As an owner, it's your job to make the right decisions for your organization. It's also your job to make sure all team members' voices are heard. And it's your job to make sure all perspectives are considered when developing new processes. Plus, it's your job to make sure every location in your company is set up with the right tools and training to execute on new processes. Finally, it's your job to ensure that new process implementation is perceived correctly and in a positive light.

If your team is not on board with the new process, then you should be concerned about your customers' perception. Having customers misperceive your new processes or policies can lead to thoughts of "Are you going out of business?" That can be very troublesome if your business relies on customers trusting they won't be left out in the cold without your service.

A good example is the trucking industry. If a trucking company goes out of business, the customer's freight might be sitting on a loading dock in the middle of nowhere with the doors shut. It could take weeks for the freight to be recovered, if at all. If customers get the perception that your company may be closing its doors soon, the trucking business may start to lose business more rapidly as customers pull out in fear that they will lose their freight.

A complete opposite example is the furniture industry. Furniture stores use the "Going Out of Business" sale all of the time as a tactic to pull people into the store. While a clearance sale like this can work short-term to help liquidate inventory to free up capital (which I do recommend), I would not recommend it as a long-term strategy. I want you to build a path to success, not a path to diminishing your brand and reputation.

You are in control of your business. You are in control of your decisions and the information you gather to make those decisions. You are in control of the perception. When making changes to your business, you need to be prepared to face criticism. It is your job to put a positive spin on changes. At times, the mismanaged perception can grow into frustration with your team. In the next pin, we will discuss how to handle that frustration of just wanting to fire everyone and start over.

**Exercise**

On a scale of 0-10 (10 being the best): Overall, how do you feel you and your team manage perception? Why did you give yourself that score?

_____

_____

_____

_____

_____

_____

_____

If you could go back to the beginning of when the business was built, what would you do differently to affect customers' perceptions? Do you feel you are in a position to change that perception now? If not, why not?

_____

_____

_____

_____

_____

_____

_____

_____

_____

Discuss with your team members how they feel about the business' current perception by customers. What ways can you and your team improve your company's perception?

_____

_____

_____

_____

_____

_____

_____

_____

*Don't forget to post the pin numbers, questions, and your answers to social media with #saleswontsave so everyone can learn from one another.*

# Pin 10
# Can I Just Fire Everyone?

YOU CANNOT JUST fire everyone! Seriously, this is one of my most hated phrases in business and in life. I have heard this phrase uttered, yelled, and screamed too many times to count. As the owner, you need to be up to the challenge of wearing many hats while simultaneously putting others in front of you and your needs.

Owning a business is hard! If it were easy, everyone would have a business. The "All or Nothing" mentality rarely ends well, and more times than not, another way exists to accomplish goals. Many times, you will find that you are just too close to the situation to see the alternative options available.

*Super Joe Says:*

*There is always another way;*

*just keep looking.*

Again, no, you cannot just fire everyone at once. But a good place to start, when you get to this point of frustration, is to look at the specific tasks each team member is set up to complete. A survey sent to your team members to find out what each of them actually does within his or her role is a great way to get a feel for what is actually going on in your business. The idea of the survey can be a great tool to use once a year. The survey can track your organization's progress and development and how roles change from year to year.

As a leader in your organization, it is your duty to make sure you know what each and every position does. You are not always expected to be a master at the positions you are responsible for, but at least this way you or another team member can fill in when needed without missing too many steps.

To go along with not missing a step, it's important to have a clear process for plugging others into a new position. One example of this can be to have clear record keeping between different locations. That way when someone from another location comes in to cover for a team member, he will not be lost in trying to figure out what was going on before he got there.

Some of your team will complain about having to do it, but I am willing to bet that many will list numerous little tasks they do throughout the day that they would never mention to anyone as being part of their job description or title. No one wants to be the person who turns in a nearly blank piece of paper to her boss when it comes to what she actually does in the company. Of course, if anyone does, it will give you a pretty accurate description of the importance of the role that person fills.

Once you have collected the surveys, you can start to build out your team structure based on this list of responsibilities for each of the roles. This list will give you a great starting point to look at which tasks need written processes. This way you can plug people into the positions actually needed for the organization to function.

Along the way, make sure you task yourself with taking a long, hard look at your hiring process. This is your first line of defense against, "Everyone sucks at his job! I guess we should just fire everyone!" You can refer back to Pin 10 for more on avoiding this pitfall.

To reiterate, no, you can't just fire everyone! What you can do instead is plan around removing team members one at a time. By building out a predictable process, you will know what steps come next when it comes to letting team members go. Knowing what the company's future will look like is important. To go along with predicting the future, in the next pin, I will discuss how to improve your scheduling skills! But first, an exercise!

### Exercise

On a scale of 0-10 (10 being the best): Overall, how do you feel you handle the termination of team members? Provide an example to explain why you gave yourself that score.

_____

_____

_____

_____

_____

_____

_____

_____

_____

How would you ideally like to go about terminating team

members?

_____

_____

_____

_____

_____

_____

_____

_____

_____

_____

_____

Do you feel your current process for plugging in team members when one is absent is working for your business? If not, why?

_____

_____

_____

_____

_____

_____

_____

_____

Discuss with your team how they feel when they have to cover for another team member. What ways can you and your team increase the standardization of record keeping and communication to make things easier when a team member is absent?

_____

_____

_____

_____

_____

_____

_____

_____

_____

*Don't forget to post the pin numbers, questions, and your answers to social media with #saleswontsave so everyone can learn from one another.*

# Pin 11
## How Do I Know If I'm on Time?

I F YOU HAVE not already started using a calendar to manage your meetings and reminders, then you need to start. Keeping a schedule for your outside appointments makes sense, and you are most likely already doing that. I want you to give some thought to how effective that has been for you. If you are a master at scheduling for yourself, have you done anything to help your team get better at scheduling?

*Super Joe Says:*
*Time is the most valuable resource;*
*more cannot be bought or created.*

Do you require your team to use a calendar program or service? Having your team all on the same page when it comes to scheduling will help save time and increase efficiency. Not only will it make it easier for your team members to schedule with each other, but they will all know where everyone is at all times. Online calendar apps and scheduling tools can cost little money or be free, depending on how big your team and its needs are.

If you have a private meeting space like a conference room, that's a great reason to use a scheduling program or app. Everyone will then be on the same page when it comes to who is scheduled to hold meetings in the conference room. Enforcing that team members must use the scheduling program to have access to the room may take a little bit of time. You can refer to Pin 17: How Do I Deal with Ruffled Feathers on My Team? to learn more about dealing with team members who dislike change. Some scheduling programs can be totally free like Google Calendar (google.com/calendar), Calendly (calendly.com), and Doodle (doodle.com).

Giving your team the ability to easily schedule, see others' schedules, and send meeting invites to customers creates a positive and predictable customer and team experience. In the next pin, I will discuss how to create an amazing customer experience that will ensure your customers keep coming back for more. Also, to go along with increasing your team's communication, I have added Pin 17, which is another opportunity for you to help increase your team's communication. Now let's finish this short pin with an exercise so you can reflect on your and your team's scheduling abilities.

**Exercise**

On a scale of 0-10 (10 being the best): How well do you feel you use scheduling skills to communicate to the rest of your team? Why did you give yourself that score?

_____

_____

_____

_____

_____

What can you do to increase your team's ability to use scheduling? How could increasing the use of scheduling help correct communication issues in your organization?

_____

_____

_____

_____

_____

_____

_____

_____

Discuss with your team the current use of scheduling. Write and discuss reasons for and against increasing the use of calendars.

_____

_____

_____

_____

_____

_____

_____

_____

_____

_____

_____

_____

_____

_____

_____

*Don't forget to post the pin numbers, questions, and your*

*answers to social media with #saleswontsave so everyone can*

*learn from one another.*

# Part 2
# Focus on the Offer

# Pin 12
# What Can a Great Customer Experience Do for My Team?

CONSISTENCY IS THE backbone of great business. Both customers and team members function better when consistency is applied. One of the best examples of consistency is a restaurant's ability to give you the same quality meal no matter who is cooking, when it is being cooked, and what location it is being ordered at. Having the same meal come out within an acceptable and expectable degree of margin for error makes customers confident in your product because they always know what they will get. The same expectation can be said for your business, no matter what industry you are in. This idea of consistency needs to be carried over into the care you give when creating processes and systems for your organization.

Creating a consistent and predictable experience for your customers is imperative if you want them to keep coming back and spreading the word about your business. You can do several things to create a positive consistency. Look for ways your business can offer value outside of what your standard service and products offer.

One way we were able to offer extra value at my family's business, Pardo's Truck Service Parts Warehouse, Inc., was by offering free training classes. We would work deals with our vendors and manufacturers to come out to our locations and provide free training and clinics to our customers. Of course, food was part of the draw; we always made sure to bring top-notch local food to the table. No one wants to learn or listen on an empty stomach!

As I mentioned in Pin 2, another way we brought value to the customer experience was once a year we would have our Annual Truck Parts Show. The manufacturers and vendors we worked with would bring their booths every year, for one night, to a huge catering location near our flagship location. This would be an opportunity for our customers to come out and network with each other, meet representatives and executives from our manufacturers, see upcoming product offerings, get free training clinics and, of course, get some top-notch food. To go along with the excellent food choices, we always had a completely free open bar. These events would draw in nearly 1,000 people in around six hours. This event was legendary here in the Northeast, and while it was imitated by competitors, I can confidently say it was never copied in scale or scope.

Want to find out how well you are creating a consistent service, product, environment, or experience for your customers and team? Start by creating a solid, but concise, list of questions to get feedback. Having social proof online with reviews is great for helping bring customers into your business, but you need more in-depth feedback. Create room in your budget that allows you to incentivize your customers to give feedback, whether that is through free gifts, gift cards, or something else outside the box.

*Super Joe Says:*

*Detailed feedback allows you to improve.*

*Take the time to communicate with your customers.*

Having the candid feedback of your customers should help open your eyes to new possibilities, new issues, and even possible solutions. Being open to feedback will play into your hand because it creates the perception that you are willing to go the extra mile to find and correct issues in your business. However, you need to be careful that you aren't all talk and no action when it comes to feedback and reviews. Ignoring on-line reviews is never a good response. Of course, there will always be trolls out there who want to tear down everything and anything they can, but having a strong professional stance on responding to negativity is important for taking the high road and giving a positive perception to other potential customers. By not responding or taking action, you will leave customers wondering whether you are really listening or care at all.

Now that you have a better understanding of what a great customer experience can do for your team, I want you to take some time to reflect with this next exercise. Then, in the next pin, I will discuss how to battle with perfection.

**Exercise**

On a scale of 0-10 (10 being the best): How well do you feel your business does at creating a great experience? Why is that your belief?

_____

_____

_____

_____

_____

_____

_____

_____

In what areas do you feel you could improve your customer experience? What goals could you set to increase your customer experience?

———————————————————————

———————————————————————

———————————————————————

———————————————————————

———————————————————————

———————————————————————

———————————————————————

———————————————————————

———————————————————————

———————————————————————

———————————————————————

———————————————————————

———————————————————————

———————————————————————

Discuss with your team the current customers' experience from the team's perspective. Write and discuss opportunities for growth in the customer experience.

_____

_____

_____

_____

_____

_____

_____

_____

_____

_____

_____

*Don't forget to post the pin numbers, questions, and your answers to social media with #saleswontsave so everyone can learn from one another.*

# Pin 13
# What Do I Do If I Feel Everything Is Perfect?

WHEN WAS THE last time you took a good hard look at your business without rose-colored glasses? Start with the outside appearance of your building. How inviting and appealing is it? Would passing traffic be enticed to stop in? Does any landscaping need to be maintained? How is your sign looking? Does it need to be touched up or even replaced? Is your sign still an accurate representation of what your business currently offers? Maybe it's time for the front of your building to get a power wash or even be repainted?

Always be looking for ways to increase your customer experience. Often, increasing the experience doesn't mean you need to spend a ton of money.

Have you looked at increasing your offering's perceived value? Often, small tweaks to how you present your offer can increase its value. Enhancing the presentation of your offering can enable you to increase your price and your overall value at the same time. One example would be to compare Six Flags to Disney in terms of the level of detail of their theme parks. Another example would be a restaurant having food just plopped on a plate, rather than plated to be more appealing. When I ordered guacamole at two different restaurants, one came out in a great looking mortar while the other restaurant came out in a big black cup that looked like it could hold any condiments (ketchup, mustard, etc.). Both restaurants had amazing guacamole, but can you guess which one was able to charge $12 and which one charged $9? Not only did I receive less for the $9 one, but it did not have the same effect as the $12 guacamole. Upgrading the presentation could greatly increase its perceived value and experience.

Marketing your offering is key for getting customers to buy into what you have to offer. Take a closer look at how you are marketing your offerings to customers who are already at your business. Do you have too few, too small, or too many signs? Think about how the outside of your building looks. Is it covered in advertising for your vendors, or can you see right through the windows into an inviting environment? It's easy to get carried away with such fluff and not realize how it is hurting your customer's experience and perception of your place of business.

*Super Joe Says:*

*Showing that you care in ways that the customer will notice goes a long way toward improving perception.*

Once you step inside your building, is the line of sight good so your team will see incoming customers? Are the shelves dusted with inventory clearly laid out in a way that makes sense for your customers to window shop? Are there products lined up against the wall behind your counter area? That was always an issue for my team because we would get so busy no one had time to leave the counter area to return items to their proper places in the warehouse.

Now look up at the lighting in your building. Are there burnt-out bulbs? Maybe it's time to replace entire fixtures or even add more fixtures?

Don't let your phone system and how customers are handled through it be an afterthought. Scrutinize the menu options your customers are presented with when they call your business. Keep the menu options limited to as few as possible for ease of use. Put a system in place to encourage your team members to update their voicemail messages frequently. Also push them to check for new messages as often as possible. You can help ensure they check their messages by picking a phone system that makes it easy for them to know when they have a new message. Make sure your on-hold music is appropriate for your customer base. Be sure to check the volume level on different types of phones so it's not too loud.

The same concerns go for office areas. It's easy to overlook things until they completely do not work, like lights. Do your team members straighten up their desks at the end of every day?

Speaking of office space, are you still using lots of filing cabinets everywhere? If that's the case, it's time to start digitizing your business to save space, time, and money. If you refuse to let go of your filing system, that's fine, but give some consideration to what those filing cabinets look like. Are they all rusted and barely functioning because they are super-old? Maybe it's time to go to a second-hand shop and get ones that actually work, are not all rusted, and hopefully match. While you're at it, make sure all of your furniture, at the bare minimum, also matches.

All of these little changes will improve your team, outside representatives, and customers' perceptions of your business. Ultimately, this raised perception will increase your profits because your business will have a look and feel that embodies character, comfort, and culture. Great first impressions are what will leave a lasting impression. So, finally, make sure your bathrooms are clean too; no one wants to poop surrounded by poop. While you are at it, make sure you are getting high-quality toilet paper.

Ultimately, I want you to create a space that truly makes you proud. Your business is your domain; it's your house that you regularly welcome people into. All too often, it's forgotten how important it is to visitors to have a space that looks like you care.

The stresses of running a business will inherently get in the way of making decisions to upgrade your appearance. For this reason, budget for these types of upgrades as you go along. Then you won't need to stretch your dollars or stress all at once to improve or expand your interior and exterior space. You just need to plan for these types of upgrades.

How easy are you making the buying experience for your customers? Have you simplified the buying process down to just asking a few simple questions to find out exactly what the customer is looking to achieve? Please remember that many customers may not have used products or services like those you have to offer, so they may not know what questions to ask or what level of quality they need, especially if your services or products are a one-time type of purchase.

Once you have made the decision to upgrade your experience for your customers and team members, you need to make sure you follow through. Just like with anything you learn, action needs to be taken on it, and it needs to be followed through on in order for it to make any difference.

In the next pin, we will cover how to increase your sales and profit through boosting your offering. But first, an exercise.

**Exercise**

On a scale of 0-10 (10 being the best): How close to perfection do you feel your organization is? Why did you give that score?

———————————————————————

———————————————————————

———————————————————————

———————————————————————

———————————————————————

———————————————————————

What areas do you feel you could improve upon in your business to get closer to perfection?

_____

_____

_____

_____

_____

_____

_____

_____

Discuss with your team members where they feel the organization is at on a scale of 0 to 10 (10 being the best) in terms of being close to perfection. Discuss and write down why they feel the organization is or isn't perfect and what can be improved upon.

_____

_____

_____

_____

_____

_____

_____

_____

_____

_____

_____

_____

_____

_____

_____

_____

_____

*Don't forget to post the pin numbers, questions, and your answers to social media with #saleswontsave so everyone can learn from one another.*

# Pin 14
# How Do I Charge More for What I Offer?

UNDERSTANDING YOUR BUSINESS' value proposition and what you are truly offering to your customers can be difficult to see at first. Taking a look at what you are really offering can be a window into how your business can increase its profit while simultaneously increasing customer satisfaction and overall trust. Low-cost add-ons can increase your bottom-line by allowing you to charge more for your goods or services. Add-ons that can boost the customer experience include enhancing the presentation, increased customer communication, and added value to the offering. Identifying where your value offering is weak is key to determining where you can increase the overall experience, price to the customer, and your ability to attract more customers.

*Super Joe Says:*

*Understand the value you are providing.*

In many cases, a business' value proposition lies in providing trust and communication. Customers want to feel like they are getting what they are paying for. They need to feel safe in assuming you are going to show up to perform the service. That means looking professional, using professional tools and techniques, communicating and acting professionally, and knowing how to respond to questions you do not have the answer for in a professional manner. If the customer feels for any reason that you are not going to show up in any way, shape, or form, then he or she will immediately start to question your fee compensation.

An example of this would be having a moving company but showing up out of uniform with a rented truck. What trust will the customer then have in that company? At that point, anyone who did not read the online reviews or word of mouth about how great you are will immediately call into question whether his stuff will wind up where he wants it to in a timely manner. The main reason for this doubt is because the moving company does not appear to be very invested in the company it is proposing to sell you on. Having great service without the professional perception will ultimately lead to the moving company needing to charge less for its services to gain customers. Showing that you have skin in the game can mean the difference between high- and low-paying customers.

Commodity goods and services will always have low profit margins, so you need to look beyond what is the low-hanging, low-profit-margin fruit your business has to offer and find another way to increase your profit on it. It could be a simple change in your offering or as complex as coming up with a whole new formula for making money with those loss leaders.

Don't be afraid to play around with your offering. Don't be afraid to ask for feedback from your customers or team. Don't be afraid to do your research and implement it to your fullest ability. Finally, don't be afraid to start with the minimal viable offering on something you have not done or offered before to test your market.

In short, don't allow fear to keep you from progress. In the next pin, I will discuss how to stay on top of your pricing. Now for an exercise on charging more for your offering.

## Exercise

On a scale of 0-10 (10 being the best): How well do you feel you are charging fair, competitive rates for your offerings? Why did you give yourself that score?

_____

_____

_____

_____

_____

On which of your offerings would you like to increase the value proposition? Why?

_____

_____

_____

_____

_____

_____

Discuss with your team the current value proposition of your offering. Write and discuss how you could increase the value proposition for your customers.

_____

_____

_____

_____

_____

_____

_____

_____

_____

*Don't forget to post the pin numbers, questions, and your answers to social media with #saleswontsave so everyone can learn from one another.*

# Pin 15
# How Do I Stay on Top of My Pricing?

WHAT ARE YOU doing for your business to stay at the forefront of pricing changes? Are you using your computer system to its fullest potential to ensure you are updating your pricing whenever it changes? Constantly be on the lookout for competitors' pricing specials so you are not blindsided by commodity items being radically cheaper. Obviously, you want to build loyalty with your customers so they're not swayed by slightly cheaper prices, but deep discounted prices will certainly sway them.

Be vigilant for bait-and-switch strategies used by competitors; for example, a competitor lists a price for a particular item, but when the item is delivered, it is not a genuine product from the manufacturer the company advertised. This can be a common practice when dealing with overly reduced pricing. The best you can do to combat this situation is working to ensure your customers are well educated on their purchases. Bad-mouthing the competition is never an acceptable solution to this problem.

Just like your customers should be doing with you, do not be afraid to ask for better pricing from your vendors. For example, you should be leveraging the amount of purchases in the past six to twelve months to negotiate a cheaper price. In some cases, you will want to take this price to market and pass the discount along to the customer, but in many cases, this rebate or price break will be where you can pick up significant profit margin. You may also want to consider not necessarily listing the cheaper price in your computer system because your sales team may then be inclined to use that lower price to win some business. However, that may make sense on a per-customer basis, so use your discretion.

*Super Joe Says:*

*A hard deal is a bad deal.*

One way to achieve deeper discounts is by looking at all of your vendors to pare down the number of vendors you purchase from. Then you will be able to increase your business' value with the vendors you retain and, in turn, give yourself more leverage. Just be aware of some of the pitfalls that can come with switching vendors. New stock keeping units (identification codes known as SKUs) can confuse your team and customers right out of the gate. Be careful to monitor for quality assurance of the new SKUs as well. Make sure to get feedback from your team and your trusted customers before making big switches.

This wraps up talking about how you can increase the value of your offer. The next pin will focus on how you can create predictable processes to increase your profit margin further.

**Exercise**

On a scale of 0-10 (10 being the best): How well do you feel you leverage your business' buying power? Why did you give yourself that score?

_____

_____

_____

_____

_____

_____

What could you improve upon to increase your buying power? Which vendors would you consider eliminating in order to increase your purchasing power with another vendor?

_____

_____

_____

_____

_____

_____

_____

_____

Discuss with your team members how they feel about your current vendors. Discuss and write down reasons for and against shifting purchases away from specific vendors and which vendors you would move your purchasing needs to.

_____

_____

_____

_____

_____

_____

_____

_____

_____

_____

*Don't forget to post the pin numbers, questions, and your answers to social media with #saleswontsave so everyone can learn from one another.*

# Part 3
# Focus on the Process

# Pin 16
# How Do I Create Profitable and Predictable Processes?

B EFORE YOU CAN start building your predictable process-es, you need to understand:

- Why you need them

- What results you're looking to achieve

- Who the processes should be created for

- Where processes should be applied

- How they will help you, your team, and your business growth

- When you need to create them

Start with collecting data on all the tasks your team works on throughout the year. Then you can start formulating a plan of attack to build necessary systems and processes.

Don't be afraid to question everything in your business. Going through this technique to find out what needs to be streamlined will likely ruffle feathers among your team, especially if they have been a part of your organization for a long time. Remind yourself constantly why you are going through the trouble of creating processes in the first place.

Start with just one operation at a time so you don't overwhelm yourself, your team, or your customers. I use the Five Ws to discover how I can best optimize the process needed:

- **Why** is the process needed?

- **What** are the desired results?

- **Who** is involved?

- **When and Where** is the process used?

- **How** will it affect the rest of my operation?

Answering the above questions will enable you to make informed conclusions before making an informed decision.

Now write out and number each and every step in the current method used to accomplish the specific task. Observe the current method taking place. Keep an eye out for all the inefficiencies happening because you haven't been taking the time to ask, "Why?"

Once you have all the steps written, you should be able to see more clearly:

- How each step relates to the others

- Which steps are unnecessary

- Which steps can be completed together

- How reducing steps will reduce costs and time

- How advancing your technology could improve efficiency

- Where adding steps could increase efficiency, quality control, and output

Creating predictable processes is not always about conserving resources. In some cases, increased output can be a big result of optimizing your processes by adding just a few extra steps.

*Super Joe Says:*

*Life is made up of percentages. Tinkering with the numbers*

*will help you develop better plans of action*

*and, ultimately, the best decisions.*

What happens when the new processes ruffle your team members' feathers? Well, that is where the next pin can be a big help. But by now, I'm sure you are expecting an exercise.

## Exercise

On a scale of 0-10 (10 being the best): How efficient do you feel your current processes are working for your business? Why did you give yourself that score?

_____

_____

_____

_____

_____

_____

_____

_____

_____

Which processes do you feel would be most helpful to the business if they were created or better optimized? Why do you feel that way?

_____

_____

_____

_____

_____

_____

_____

_____

_____

_____

Discuss with your team the current processes they go through routinely. Discuss and write down ways you can optimize those processes, and explain why the optimization would make such a big difference.

_____

_____

_____

_____

_____

_____

_____

_____

_____

_____

_____

_____

_____

*Don't forget to post the pin numbers, questions, and your answers to social media with #saleswontsave so everyone can learn from one another.*

# Pin 17
# How Do I Deal with Ruffled Feathers on My Team?

WHAT DO YOU do when your long-time team members are afraid of the changes coming down the pike? In this situation, you need to understand the difference between brainstorming to make the system better and a team member refusing to change his or her day-to-day workflow.

Brainstorming with your team members can help improve the process you've laid out in front of them. Be aware that small issues may be overlooked when developing the revised process. These overlooked aspects can be as small as inconveniencing your team members or customers to as big as setting your team up for failure.

*Super Joe Says:*

*Allowing others to be part of building the process*

*will ensure their commitment to the process.*

As discussed earlier, you need to take into consideration your team members and customers' perception when making large changes to operations. Processes used for inventory management can have a sweeping effect over the entire business. If your team gets the impression that you no longer have inventory for your shelves, then you can expect customers to have a similar opinion.

Try to put yourself into your team members' shoes. In some cases, you may actually need to sit down and do their jobs for a short time to see the shortcomings of a new process. The tasks in question may be something you did at one time in the past, but coming at the tasks with a fresh set of eyes and more experience will make a big difference in helping you see the inefficiencies. Understanding every step of the process will help you figure out what you can remove or improve upon. You need to be committed to spending time involved in the process.

I know—it all sounds easier than it is. That's why, in

the next pin, I want to share with you what you can do when you do ruffle team members' feathers.

## Exercise

On a scale of 0-10 (10 being the best): How well do you feel you are able to put yourself in others' shoes? Why did you give yourself that score?

_____

_____

_____

_____

_____

_____

_____

_____

How do you feel you could improve your empathy?

_____

_____

_____

_____

_____

_____

_____

_____

Discuss with your team how previous changes in processes have affected their workflow. Discuss and write down ways to communicate better so you can increase performance and decrease ruffled feathers.

_____

_____

_____

_____

_____

_____

_____

*Don't forget to post the pin numbers, questions, and your answers to social media with #saleswontsave so everyone can learn from one another.*

**Pin 18**
**Joe, Do You Have a Personal Story About Ruffling Feathers?**

WHY, YES, I do! It was the end of 2011, and my family's business, Pardo's Truck Service Parts Warehouse, Inc., was faced with a cash crunch, a massive inventory issue, and a growth problem. Many changes in the trucking industry, the previous 2008 recession, the looming growth recession of 2012, and some poor business decisions in past inventory management had landed us in a tough position.

*Super Joe Says:*

*Everything pays rent for the space taken up.*

Sitting on over five million dollars in inventory at the time was also a massive issue. However, I saw this situation as an opportunity to try something new. I wanted to use my passion for processes and technology to reduce our slowest-moving inventory and increase our fastest-moving inventory. Doing so would ultimately free up cash and allow us to become more profitable. I was only twenty-five at the time and completely unprepared for the journey ahead of me and the lessons I would learn.

My grandfather, who had started the business in 1981, was never a fan of using technology to determine inventory management numbers. The minimum and maximum amounts to stock per item were set by people. A long list of a supplier's product numbers would be printed out with a limited amount of history information. Those printed history numbers and a general knowledge of the items themselves would decide the minimum and maximum amount to stock per item. After the sheets would be marked up with new min and max amounts, someone would have to sit at a computer and enter the changes to each part number by hand.

Many years earlier, I had discovered how we could manipulate our min and max stocking amounts with an algorithm. When I presented this idea to my grandfather, he told me an algorithm could not take into account that you need multiples of a number to complete a task on a truck. For example, you would need two brake shoes per wheel when doing a brake job. In that case, you would want to make sure you always had at least four shoes on the shelf so you could do two wheels at a time.

When I considered building our own custom algorithms in 2011, I looked at our monthly history for individual numbers. I noticed that many months we would sell odd numbers of parts that I was being told would only be sold in specific multiples. Based on this information, I lobbied to have the computer decide our stocking levels based on an algorithm I would create. In some cases, the parts being regularly sold in multiples would have a multiple number regardless. I did not see an issue with this, with the exception of part numbers that stocked less than two due to low sales to begin with.

Shortly into the process of changing the company's stocking amounts, I learned many of our team members were unhappy. They felt they were not being listened to, their experience was not being taken into consideration, and I, being young and maybe naïve, was trying to come in and make changes for the sake of changes. While I had been working at the company since I was six—pushing brooms, straightening shelves, counting and checking in inventory—many of our team members had been with the company since before I was born. Therefore, I was rapidly feeling the pressure of fighting an uphill battle.

My logic was built on what I considered to be a solid foundation. People can have a bad sense of time, but computers knew everything about our inventory and customers, including how long inventory had been sitting on a shelf, and the last time a specific customer purchased a specific part. However, to offset complaints, I told our managers they could order more of any part number than what the computer system told them they could stock. I understood they could never grow their inventory or sales if they only stocked what the system told them. This permission enabled our managers to be managers and the system to be flexible.

My plan was to adjust on a regular basis all of the stocking levels in the company based on how often we ordered from our vendors and how often our satellite stores would get a stock order from the main warehouse. Our business was built around a hub-and-spoke model with our central warehouse feeding all eleven locations and handling over one million dollars of incoming inventory every month. The algorithm would enable us to adjust our min and max stocking amounts on a nearly daily basis for new sales to be incorporated.

To get the ball rolling so we could free up our cash by reducing unnecessary inventory, we sent out a massive number of return sheets to our satellite locations. These returns included parts that, according to our system, had seen no sales in the previous twelve months. We could move that unused inventory to other locations that needed the inventory so they would not need to purchase more in the short term. I told our managers they were allowed to keep extra inventory they wanted and felt they needed, but obviously, they had to send some amount back. For example, if they had ten of a specific part number on the shelf and the system told them they should only have one, they could keep a few extras just in case they sold them, but I requested they still send four or five back to the main warehouse. This wiggle room enabled our managers to feel like and actually be part of the process. I didn't want to dictate to our team in an inflexible and uncompromising way.

In the beginning, one person was the most vocal against what I was trying to do. With good cause, he pushed back because of the inability to dictate to the computer system which parts needed to be stocked in multiples. This push back was good for me because it taught me to look harder for a way to solve complex issues. I could have given up and backed down on optimizing our inventory system, but instead, I pushed harder. I went back to the drawing board with our computer system supplier, and after many weeks of back and forth, I came out with a solution to calculate for multiple quantities.

For many months, I would be in our main warehouse, helping to receive excess inventory, check it in, and put it on the shelves. The quicker we were able to make this process happen, the less we would purchase from our vendors. By the late afternoon, I would be doing the paperwork to move the checked-in inventory. At night after dinner, I would be up in my home office working on the algorithm to make it as accurate for our needs as possible.

Moving forward was the most important piece to accomplishing our goals. Standing still and trying to get everything perfect on the first try would have netted zero results. That was not an option for us because we needed to free up as much cash as possible.

Two years into our shift in inventory management at Pardo's Truck Service Parts Warehouse, Inc., the results spoke for themselves. We were able to reduce our inventory value by nearly half, increase ROI (Return on Investment) by 25 percent, and increase sales in many stores by 10 percent.

The unintended result of pushing myself so hard and dealing with the criticisms over the changes was that I was completely burnt out. I felt I was ready to move on, and in the late summer of 2013, I went to my dad's house to have the most difficult conversation ever. I was ready to leave the company that my great-grandfather started over thirty years earlier. I didn't know what I was going to do with my life at the time. Fortunately, I was prepared to figure it out.

April 2, 2014 was my last day working at the company. I was ready for something else, and just one month later, I stumbled into podcasting (www.TheeBusinessPodcast.com), and the rest is history.

*Super Joe Says:*

*Sometimes, you just need to slow down.*

What did I learn from these experiences? Turning the heat up all at once on your team to get desired changes is not always the most effective way to communicate. While patience can be difficult when so much is on the line, it can allow you to go much further without getting burnt out. Always keep in mind that the possibilities are endless if you keep an open mind and are willing to put the work in. In the next pin, I'll discuss how you can keep yourself moving through fear.

**Exercise**

On a scale of 0-10 (10 being the best): How well do you feel you keep your emotions under control? Why do you give yourself that score, and if the score is low, what can you do better?

_____

_____

_____

_____

_____

_____

_____

_____

What major change have you made in your business that has ruffled feathers? How do you think you could have handled the situation better?

_____

_____

_____

_____

_____

_____

_____

_____

Discuss with your team members a time when changes to the business ruffled their feathers and how that situation could have been handled better. Then write down how you can build processes to better communicate drastic changes in the business' processes.

_____

_____

_____

_____

_____

_____

_____

_____

_____

*Don't forget to post the pin numbers, questions, and your*

*answers to social media with #saleswontsave so everyone can*

*learn from one another.*

## Pin 19
## What Do I Do If I Fear Change?

D O NOT BE afraid to try new things. Fear of the unknown will hold you and your business back from becoming great. Be willing to accept that you may need to sacrifice comfort for your business to become the next great version of itself. Start by building those processes and then putting them into place.

*Super Joe Says:*

*The old way is the foundation for the new way.*

Your new processes will not be perfect at first or even on the twentieth implementation. If your new processes do not create or unearth new issues to be solved, then you probably are not critiquing your processes hard enough. Keep the human factor involved in your new processes so your team stays involved and feels valued.

Don't forget to look to others for help and advice on solving issues. People do not need to be in your industry to have ideas on how to solve specific problems. Another option is to look at hiring a business consultant (like me) to help build processes and solve complex problems.

In life and business, it's important to keep in perspective that we are not all great at every aspect of our businesses. You probably didn't start your business because you love crunching numbers, developing processes, or working with others. Those activities will all come as a result of being successful at what you do, and you may not be as successful at doing them. Focus on what you do best and find people who can help you in your areas of weakness. Just as you may hire an accountant to do your taxes, you can hire a business consultant to help solve your business problems. The fresh set of eyes and fresh set of experience the consultant offers can help you find ways to improve your business that you may not have considered otherwise.

*Super Joe Says:*

*The world is moving forward at such a rapidly increasing pace that standing still is not an option.*

Business owners from all over the world face similar concerns every day, and many have discovered how finding a fresh set of eyes can help inspire them to find more innovative solutions. So don't be afraid to own the fact that you're not perfect. Showing up every day to solve the problems of our world is part of the experience that enables us to grow. Embrace problem-solving and see how it rewards you and your business.

Speaking of fear, in the next pin I discuss a big fear many people have—integrating technology into your business. Now for an exercise on fear.

**Exercise**

On a scale of 0-10 (10 being the best): How well do you feel you handle change? Why do you give yourself that score?

_____

_____

_____

_____

_____

What score would you give yourself for how you feel you handle fear, and why?

_____

_____

_____

_____

_____

What areas could you improve on when it comes to handling change and fear?

_____

_____

_____

_____

_____

_____

_____

_____

Discuss with your team members what fears they have when it comes to the business and change. Then write action plans to reduce fear for upcoming changes.

_____

_____

_____

_____

_____

_____

_____

*Don't forget to post the pin numbers, questions, and your answers to social media with #saleswontsave so everyone can learn from one another.*

# Pin 20
# How Can I Integrate Technology into My Business?

MANY BUSINESS PROBLEMS that need solving come down to math. If math scares you, that's okay; I totally understand, but you need to understand that computers are designed to crunch numbers and solve difficult math problems. You just need to figure out what numbers to feed into the computer to get the desired results.

Technology becomes easier to use and has more capabilities with each passing year. For example, what started out as just being able to track inventory via a keyboard now can use barcodes and even NFC (near field communication) tags. Therefore, you should take advantage of technology every chance you get.

The processes you create for your team can use technology in a complex way. However, if your processes are not simplistic enough for your team to follow along, you need to go back to the drawing board.

*Super Joe Says:*

*Simply explain simply.*

Integrating technology into most aspects of your business can give you a competitive edge over your competition. Examples of the competitive edge can be found in some of the following examples.

- GPS technology to track driver delivery routes to save fuel and time

- Inventory scanners or NFC tags for accurately moving product around your organization

- KPIs (key performance indicators) to track output from your team

- Internal company website to increase communication speed of key news

Like technology, you, your team, and your business need to be constantly ready to adapt for the changes ahead.

After the following exercise, I discuss why every leader is a professional problem solver.

**Exercise**

On a scale of 0-10 (10 being the best): How well do you feel your business harnesses technology? Why did you give yourself that score?

_____

_____

_____

_____

_____

_____

In which areas do you feel you could expand your use of technology to increase communication and team and customer satisfaction? Also, what technology have you looked into implementing but have not pulled the trigger on yet? Explain why.

_____

_____

_____

_____

_____

_____

_____

_____

_____

_____

_____

_____

_____

Discuss with your team how technology is currently implemented into the business. Also discuss how implementing new
technology would help your team. Discuss and write down a
plan to obtain and implement new technology.

_____

_____

_____

_____

_____

_____

_____

_____

_____

_____

_____

_____

_____

_____

*Don't forget to post the pin numbers, questions, and your*

*answers to social media with #saleswontsave so everyone can*

*learn from one another.*

## Pin 21
## Are the Possibilities Endless for Me Too?

*Super Joe Says:*

*If owning a business were easy,*

*everyone would do it.*

A S A LEADER, you need to remember that your job description is "Professional Problem Solver." Keep your head up, always looking forward and into the future. Having a vision for your company is imperative when crafting goals that push the business five, ten, and even twenty years into the future.

Being able to explain your vision to others is crucial to your success. Without explanation, you will find yourself stuck in one place. If you are not moving forward, you cannot grow and the world will pass you by. If you are not learning, then you are not growing. If you are not growing, then you are dying.

Figure out what you are bad, good, and great at within your business. Then you can hire your team to aid you in your weakest parts to help propel you and the business forward. Being self-aware of your strengths and weaknesses will be a game-changer for your growth.

A way always exists to achieve the results you are looking for. Anything is possible if you are willing to put the work in, dig deeper, and use people and resources more efficiently. Think beyond your current means and resources to create solutions you never thought would be possible. Don't be afraid to challenge yourself and your team every step of the way. Stay focused on the goal, but don't be afraid to come up with throwaway ideas. Those ideas can inspire better solutions to the challenges you and your team are facing.

As you create solutions to existing problems, be prepared to take on any new issues that will arise. These issues will require a deeper understanding of the processes currently being used. One of the quickest ways to solve issues and resolve stress is to have a great understanding of the numbers that most affect your business. We'll look at those numbers in the next pin.

**Exercise**

On a scale of 0-10 (10 being the best): How good do you feel you are at problem solving? Why did you give yourself that score?

_____

_____

_____

_____

_____

_____

_____

Give an example of a time you did well at problem solving in the business and a time when you came up short. What areas do you feel you could improve upon when it comes to problem solving and why?

Ask your team for feedback on your problem-solving skills. Write down what worked and what didn't work very well for your team based on your past decisions.

_____

_____

_____

_____

_____

_____

_____

_____

_____

_____

_____

*Don't forget to post the pin numbers, questions, and your answers to social media with #saleswontsave so everyone can learn from one another.*

# Pin 22
# What Numbers Should I Know?

"**K**NOW YOUR NUMBERS!" is a classic and overused phrase. However, it's vital to know your numbers—don't let knowledge of them get away from you. Much stress and frustration can stem from the guessing game that ends up being played when you don't know your numbers.

*Super Joe Says:*

*Numbers don't lie.*

You need to know how much money is coming in and going out every day, week, month, and year in order to know whether what you are doing is working. Knowing as much data as possible about your business will help take that guessing game off your plate and lighten the stress that comes with it.

Later in this pin, I have included an extensive list of definitions and formulas on how to figure out those numbers.

You need to stop the guessing game when it comes to knowing your numbers. The guessing game hurts you, your team, your business, and your customers. Once you know the basic numbers, you can start to dive in deeper. Then you can begin creating what I call "Next Gen Numbers."

Time to go beyond just knowing your numbers. Let's put them to work!

If you have your numbers in a program, it should be easy to break them down so you can see month-over-month and yearly trends. Utilizing these trends will help you get out of the guessing game and into making educated decisions based on the cold hard numbers, not what you feel.

Too often, people fall back into going with their gut feelings and what they knew to be true at one point in time. Things are changing every single day—in life and in business.

It's imperative that you stay on top of the mounting trends in your business to avoid any blindside hits.

You can use the data you've collected to make investing in your business a lot simpler because you will know and not be guessing. Expanding and contracting areas of focus for your business will be leaps and bounds easier when you have the data laid out in front of you.

When was the last time you set sales goals for your business? You've heard that question before, I'm sure, but I want you to take it one step further. Instead of just stating that you want to hit X sales goals for a period, track it and give periodic updates to your team based on the data available. That way your team can stay on task and on track to meet those goals. Tracking will also enable conversation on how to meet those goals. Without those conversations, you aren't giving your team a clear path to success, which is a quick way to wind up having unmet expectations and all-around disappointment.

Try to keep your goals obtainable and reasonable so you can use them as a springboard of encouragement for you and your team. Small wins are wins. You don't have to swing for the fences for a homerun every time you go to set goals. Increases and decreases of 5 to 10 percent over specific time periods should be reasonable. Setting such reasonable goals will also help with combating big downturns if you land business that is a one-and-done deal. Next, we can move on to creating your own Next Gen Numbers.

## How Can I Create Next Gen Numbers?

Next Gen Numbers can be set for every position in your business and are different in every industry. They will help you track inefficiencies, which will save you money and add profit to your bottom line.

One example of a Next Gen Number I created and used was to track the accuracy of our stock pickers in our central warehouse. Every day, hundreds of parts were picked off our central warehouse shelves to be sent to our satellite stores for stock and specific orders. We used a scanner and barcode system to create orders for the satellite stores that in theory should have been 100 percent accurate. As we quickly found out, that was far from the case.

Some members of our warehouse team were much more accurate in their scanning than others. The day after the inventory was sent, we would receive the corrections back. From there, I kept a running tally in a spreadsheet that gave team members a percentage score on their accuracy individually and as a whole. Based on this data, we determined we were able to lower our percentage of shipping errors out of our warehouse.

When it comes to figuring out what to track to base your Next Gen Numbers on, you have to look at what data you have available to you. What data can you extract from the daily process you already have going on in your business? Once you decide what to track, you just need to keep a record of it in a spreadsheet. It doesn't need to be a super-complex spreadsheet, but gather as many data points as possible to help you build an average and, most importantly, an expectation. Once you have that base line of numbers, you can start to build an expectation and build predictions for how changes in your current process will affect the numbers. The results will most likely surprise you!

Once you have your basic numbers tracked and have goals built around them, you'll be able to start finding and tracking these Next Gen Numbers to start the process of building your business into a well-oiled machine.

Here's an outline of the basic numbers you should know to make educated decisions and help build your Next Gen Numbers.

### Expenses

Money spent in order to generate revenue.

### Expense Target

Projected goal of the total expenses incurred during a specified time period.

## Revenue

Income generated from sales.

## Revenue Target

Projected goal of the total revenue during a specified time period.

## Cost of Goods Sold

Cost of obtaining materials and creating the finished goods that are sold.

Formula: Beginning Merchandise Inventory + Net Purchases of Merchandise – Ending Merchandise Inventory

## Profit

The surplus of money after total costs are deducted from total revenue.

Formula: (Revenue – Cost) / Revenue x 100

## Profit Margin

Percentage of profit left after taxes.

Formula: After-Tax Profit x 100 / Cost of Sales

## Net Profit

Total earned or lost in a specified time period. Formula: Total Expenses – Total Revenue

## Gross Profit

Difference between revenue and cost of goods. Formula: Revenue – Total Expenses

## Debt

Obligation to pay money.

## Accounts Receivable

Amount of sales not yet paid for by customers.

## Accounts Payable

Unpaid bills.

## Return on Investment (ROI)

A percentage that compares profitability or efficiency of investments.

Formula: (Net Profit / Total Investment) x 100

## Stock Turnover

Number of times inventory is replenished during a specific period.

Formula: Cost of Sales / Average Inventory

## Sales

While it can be talked about as revenue, you should also know the number of units sold and the average number of transactions in a given period.

## Sales Closing Rate

Percentage of prospects who become paying customers.

Formula: (Number of Successful Sales / Number of Leads) x 100

## Average Time to Collect

The average amount of time it takes to collect your accounts receivables.

## Salaries

Amount you are paying your team members in specific roles.

## Cost of Customer Acquisition

Amount of expenses in marketing to acquire one customer.

Formula: Marketing Expenses / Number of Customers Acquired

## How Do I Increase My Profit?

Now that you have gone through all of your numbers and even created new numbers to help, we can look at balancing your sales mix and examining ways to plus-up your current offer.

First, look at what percentage is coming from high-profit margin versus low-profit margin sales.

Now, take a look at how much you are spending on high-profit margin sales versus low-profit margin sales. This comparison will help you gauge how you can better spend your money and create a game plan for how you are going to inject more high-profit margin sales into your mix. Allocating money for specific items in proportion to your overall budget will give you insight into where best to spend your capital.

Getting your mix right can include branching out into bringing more product lines together. You need to be careful, though, that you are not spending too much of your budget on betting whether a new product will take off with your customers. Identifying great add-on sales items that come with high-profit margins is key to bolstering your overall profit margin. Don't be scared to try something new, but make sure you educate your team on the benefits of selling the new products. If you have their support and they are educated, you are increasing your new products' potential success.

*Super Joe Says:*

*Always be looking for percentages*

*so you can measure even the tiniest success.*

It's always easier to sell to existing customers than to find new ones. Getting feedback from your customers on what they would like to get from your business is always helpful for making more informed decisions. You can achieve that feedback in many different ways from just straight out asking the right questions to giving out surveys. You will most likely get opinions from the happiest or unhappiest people, so you will need to set up the survey to give you an average.

I know I packed a ton into this pin. I hope the examples, definitions, and ideas will resonate with you and encourage you to take action. Next, in the final note, I discuss what it takes to become successful.

**Exercise**

On a scale of 0-10 (10 being the best): How well do you know your numbers? How confident are you in your numbers? Explain why you gave yourself that score.

_____

_____

_____

_____

_____

What numbers do you need to have a better understanding
of? How can understanding your numbers help you?

_____

_____

_____

_____

_____

_____

_____

_____

_____

Discuss with your team the possibility of creating Next Gen Numbers. Discuss and write down which Next Gen Numbers you can come up with.

_____

_____

_____

_____

_____

_____

_____

_____

_____

_____

_____

_____

_____

_____

*Don't forget to post the pin numbers, questions, and your answers to social media with #saleswontsave so everyone can learn from one another.*

# A Final Note
# How Do I Become Successful?

I N ORDER TO become successful, first you must define your vision of your success. Doing so will allow you to set the goals for you, your team, and your business going into the future. Start with what you want your life and business to look like in five, ten, and twenty years. It's often easier to start with your desired destination and work backward to figure out how you'll get there. This backward process enables you to uncover the milestones you will need to pass in order to reach your ultimate goals.

No one sees the world like you do. You need to own your vision every step of the way. There will always be people who challenge you on what you are looking to accomplish. Work on understanding and refining your vision to the point where you become fearless enough to tell others about it.

*Super Joe Says:*

*No one will love you as much as*

*you need to love yourself.*

I hope *Sales Won't Save Your Small Business* has provided you with the tools you need to become successful or to take your success to the next level. But to do that, you need to take ac-tion. That action might begin with going back and reread-ing this book to get clear on anything you still have questions about. It definitely should include completing all the exercises I created for you. Then you need to take specific action on what you have learned. Don't worry; you don't have to do it all alone. You have your team members to help you, and you can always reach out to me for help or clarification. You'll find my contact information at the end of this book.

I wish you much success in not only saving your busi-ness but in taking it to the next level.

# Who Is This Super Joe Guy Anyway?

SUPER JOE PARDO is a New Jersey-based, sixth generation business owner who works with businesses and owners to help them grow by focusing on their teams, offers, and processes.

Born in 1986, just five years into Pardo's existence, it seemed like destiny that Joe would work there and eventually take it over. The path to that destiny, however, was paved with twists and turns, one of the most profound twists coming at the age of seven.

At the time, Joe decided he didn't want to take over the family business because he wanted to be a child psychiatrist to help other kids like him who were dealing with divorce. His grandparents told him it didn't matter what he wanted to be when he grew up because as long as he did the best job he could, they would be proud of him. That would forever change his life.

As time went on, Joe decided to stay and work in the family business, and he is forever grateful for the business and life lessons he learned during his time there—not to mention all of the amazing people who became like family to him and remain so to this day.

Over the more than two decades Joe spent in the company, he worked in or alongside every position in the company, including:

1. Warehouse Employee

2. Counterman

3. Information Technologies Director

4. Salesman

5. Director of Operations

In 2014, he decided to leave his family's $100 million business, Pardo's Truck Service Parts Warehouse, Inc., to pursue his dreams of starting his own business. Shortly after, he created the award-winning show, *The Business Podcast Featuring Super Joe Pardo*. The podcast provides business lessons from business owners around the world. Joe's platform is based on helping business owners pursue the businesses and lifestyles of their dreams.

Find out more about Joe at

SuperJoePardo.com!

# What Was Pardo's Truck Service Parts Warehouse, Inc.?

FOUNDED IN 1981 by Joseph R. Pardo, Pardo's Truck Service Parts Warehouse, Inc. originally operated in a 1,500 sq. ft. building. Today, it has grown to an eleven-store operation, with its flagship location boasting a 45,000 sq. ft. building. Its corporate headquarters is located in Deptford, New Jersey, which is also home to its distribution warehouse and parts store consisting of a 4,000 sq. ft. showroom.

Pardo's serviced the Mid-Atlantic seaboard area from Philadelphia to Washington, DC, including the eastern shore of Maryland. With the start of a new millennium, Pardo's expanded in 2000 to the west coast of Florida to serve the Tampa, Sarasota market. G.B.S., LLC, formally Guys Brake Service of Pennsauken, New Jersey, was acquired in 2002, adding another company to its family. In 2006, Pardo's acquired Goldie's Truck Parts in Kearny, New Jersey, extending its services to the northern New Jersey market. In 2008, Pioneer Truck Sales in Washington Township, New Jersey, became part of the Pardo family; it does installations and repairs.

When Pardo's Truck Service Parts Warehouse, Inc. was sold to FleetPride in early 2015, Pardo's was a leader in supplying the transportation industry. Pardo's always had a commitment to having the parts its customers needed in stock. It accomplished this goal in part by tailoring its inventory to its customer base and market. It was committed to its customers having a positive and satisfying experience when dealing with Pardo's.

# Hire Super Joe Pardo to Take Your Business to the Next Level

HAVE YOU READ *Sales Won't Save Your Small Business* but you still want more personal help relevant to specify your business and its unique needs?

Then look no further. Super Joe Pardo is ready to help you change your bottom line worries into business successes.

Joe has spent four years doing business consulting. He has helped over thirty kinds of companies....

Joe knows you need practical results. He will go over your numbers with you, walk through your business with you, and even help you create those Next Gen Numbers you need to succeed. His approach is a customized experience because every business is unique!

Contact Joe Pardo today for a complimentary fifteen-minute call so he can learn more about you and your business and how he can help you meet your needs.

Joe@SuperJoePardo.com

(609) 868-9301

SuperJoePardo.com

# Book Super Joe Pardo to Speak at Your Next Event

SUPER JOE PARDO has been wowing audiences for the last four years with his speeches directed at how you can motivate your team members to increase your sales and improve your bottom line.

As the host of the award-winning *The Business Podcast Featuring Super Joe Pardo,* Joe has the experience and knowledge your audience needs and the ability to deliver it succinctly and in a humorous yet educational way.

Whether your audience is 10 or 10,000, in North America or abroad, Joe Pardo can create a tailored speech that will leave your audience or team members inspired and ready to take their businesses to the next level.

For a free interview with Joe about how he can help your audience, contact him today.

Joe@SuperJoePardo.com

(609) 868-9301

SuperJoePardo.com

If You Enjoyed *Sales Won't Save Your Small Business*, You'll Love

# Super Joe Pardo's Other Books

## Joe Pardo's 31 Life-Changing Concepts

JOE PARDO WROTE *31 Life-Changing Concepts* because he strives every day to live by these concepts. How this self-development book is written is important because Joe is a slow reader and does not read many books. A short and intentional book with no fluff was the goal. Joe's hand-drawn pictures were done with Sharpies to show the power of what someone who "isn't an artist" can accomplish. The message here is simple: Be Yourself!

## How to Dream Big and Win

A COLORING BOOK DESIGNED as a map to help you figure out what your dreams are and how to make them your reality. Joe feels coloring will help you reconnect with your inner kid and childhood dreams. This will lead to a clear path to obtain success and more importantly happiness!

### *iSelf Empower: 160 Self Affirmations to Empower You*

THIS BOOK IS the result of a dream Joe had on April 18, 2017. He woke up around 10 p.m. to start outlining the powerful "I statements" in it. One week later, the book was complete. It's a book that punches people in the face with positive, reflective, and repetitive messaging to build confidence and help you own your life.

*iSelf Empower* will inspire you to take your life to the next level. Keep an open mind because this book is unlike any other. There are even some surprises hidden in plain sight.

**All of Super Joe Pardo's books are available at Amazon.**

www.ingramcontent.com/pod-product-compliance
Lightning Source LLC
Chambersburg PA
CBHW071256220526
45468CB00001B/146